The
Prophetic
Almanac
2022

By
Pastor Bill Jenkins

The Prophetic Almanac 2022

By Pastor Bill Jenkins

Manufactured in the
United States of America
ISBN # 978-0-578-32736-5

Published by
B&B Media
Upland, California
Visit the author's website at:
www.pastorbilljenkins.org

TABLE OF CONTENTS

INTRODUCTION

There are 31,102 scriptures in the Bible and every word is important. Every word is valuable. Every word is perfectly placed and put in scripture for a purpose. The Bible is the inerrant, infallible, and inspired Word of God.

> *"All scripture is given by inspiration of God, and is profitable for doctrine, for reproof, for correction, for instruction in righteousness: That the man of God may be perfect, thoroughly furnished unto all good works." 2 Timothy 3:16-17*

So, if every word is supposed to be in the Word, then there is a reason certain colors, symbols, and numbers are mentioned in the scripture. There are no accidents in the Bible. Each color, symbol, and number is put in scripture on purpose and our job is to search for a connection and look for a meaning based on the consistency of its use in the Bible.

> *"It is the glory of God to conceal a thing: but the honour of kings is to search out a matter." Proverbs 25:2*

God wants us to be so in love with Him and so passionate about knowing Him more that we search

1

the scriptures to find out hidden knowledge about Him. That is what this book is all about.

I want to be clear that what I am giving you is not a spiritual guess or some weird Christian calculation in order to release some new revelation. I am also not trying to sanctify numerology. Christianity and the occult do not go together any more than Christianity and murder. This is only a sincere effort to know God and His plans more by studying scripture using a method of understanding the meaning of numbers in the Bible in order to accomplish that goal.

It is also important to note that this is not a book that is full of my feelings, thoughts, and opinions for the vision in the coming year. It is not even a book where I am writing things that I feel "led" of the Lord to give you as I was in the presence of the Lord. I have spent hundreds of hours studying and listening to the Lord to find out what He wants for us this year. This is a book where I am releasing the vision for 2022 based upon my personal study of the number 22 and its nine mentions in scripture. I have followed the facts and allowed my study to take me where it did. I have stayed true to the content and context of what I have come across in the Word in order to release a genuine road map to navigate our way in the year to come. I think everything in this book is cool, but my favorite part is where I look at every book of the Bible that has a chapter 22 in it.

Although there are three main things that 22 revolves around when it is mentioned nine times in scripture, the revelation that comes from the chapter 22's of the Bible will give you further insight on what 2022 will bring. This book is full of information, inspiration, and divine revelation. It is important to start a new year with a new vision of hope that is directed by the Holy Spirit. We need to know what to expect from God and what God expects of us. This vision is not intended to please people or bring encouragement that will fade when "life" comes at you and hits you hard during the year. I want this prophetic Word to last all 365 days of 2022 and release "God things," not just "good things." The integrity that comes in understanding the significance of the number 22 in the Bible will sustain you through all the attacks of the enemy.

> *"But he answered and said, It is written, Man shall not live by bread alone, but by every word that proceedeth out of the mouth of God." Matthew 4:4*

It is what it is!!! The Word of God says what it says. Do not just reject things you do not understand. By the same token, do not just accept it all without testing it through the lens of the Bible. I dare you to go deeper and higher in your walk with Jesus. Do not settle for an ankle deep, knee deep, or even a waist deep relationship with God. Be willing to go further and venture out into diverse ways that can develop your relationship with the Lord.

This is going to be a unique year with a lot of twists and turns, but God has not brought you this far to abandon you now. Be willing to risk a little in order to gain a great reward. This vision is designed to give you true insight as to what is to come in 2022. Use this book to help you understand what God is up to and what He is doing to prepare you for the soon coming of the Lord. You are not living in the last days. You are living in the last of the last days. So, jump in, trust God, and get ready for the ride of a lifetime! Do not let fear keep you from being everything God wants you to be in 2022.

CHAPTER 1
2022 Preview

This year will be a year like no other. So, get ready for a preview of the most important year of your life. A preview of something is designed to create enthusiam by releasing inside information of what is to come in the future. Previews do not give you everything you need to know, but they give you enough information to make a more educated decision. The preview of this year will provide the necessary tools for you to understand what God is up to and what God expects from you in 2022.

Sports of the Year
NFL and Soccer
Both sports have 22 players on the field at all times

State of the Year
Alabama is the 22nd state that came into the Union on December 14, 1819

City of the Year
Detroit, Michigan

Planet of the Year
Mars

Bible Characters of the Year

Women = Ruth, she was an educator of loyalty
Men = Ahab, he was a tolerator of bad behavior
Youth = Samson, he was a rejector of godly advice

Bible Story of the Year

Ruth and Boaz's marriage in Ruth 4
Their relationship shows the importance of how
serving one another leads to success.

Scripture of the Year

*"And when he had said this, he breathed
on them, and saith unto them, Receive ye
the Holy Ghost:" John 20:22*

Book of the Bible of the Year

Lamentations
This book has a total of five chapters. Four of the
chapters have 22 verses. Chapter 3 has 66 verses,
which is 22 x 3. The book is basically about how
Jeremiah is mourning over the sin in the land.

Fruit of the Spirit

Patience

Gift of the Spirit for the Year

Prophecy

Word of the Year
Covenant

Color of the Year
Ebony
Ebony is a dark black

Super Food of the Year
Strawberries

Vegetable of the Year
Broccoli

Snack of the Year
Coconut

Geographical Places of the Year
- China
- Russia
- Sudan
- Dominican Republic
- Columbia
- Cuba
- Gulf of Mexico
- Great Britain

Animal of the Year
Lion

Lions are symbols of strength and courage. They have been celebrated as animal royalty and they are known as the "King of the Jungle." Lions are mentioned over 100 times in scripture. Jesus is referred to as the "Lion of Judah" in Revelation 5:5. Daniel was thrown into a den of lions and was almost eaten by a lion in Daniel 6:16-24 until God made a way and gave the lions lock jaw. The devil is also referred to as a "roaring lion" in 1 Peter 5:8, but he is a counterfeit. The lion is a beautiful and strong animal. Lions are a picture of Christ.

Characteristics of a Lion

<u>Positive</u>	<u>Negative</u>
- Family-oriented	- Fighters
- Great night vision	- Lack endurance
- Social	- Intolerant
- Superb hunters	- Over-eaters
- Good communicators	- Territorial
- Can climb	- Sneaky & deceptive
- Protective	- Destructive
- Fast	- Prideful
- Good parents	- Big heads
- Do not seek approval	- Loud
- Never back down	- Like to be alone and isolated
- Determined	- Intimidate others with their roar
- Fearless	- Inactive during the day

22 Movies of the Year

1. Morbius (January)
2. Uncharted (February)
3. The Batman (March)
4. Lost City of D (March)
5. Bullet Train (April)
6. Fantastic Beasts and Where to Find Them 3 (April)
7. John Wick: Chapter 4 (May)
8. Top Gun 2 (May)
9. DC League of Super-Pets (May)
10. Doctor Strange in the Multiverse of Madness (May)
11. Jurassic World: Dominion (June)
12. Black Adam (July)
13. Thor: Love and Thunder (July)
14. Samaritan (August)
15. The Man from Toronto (August)
16. Mission: Impossible 7 (September)
17. Spider-Man: Into the Spider-Verse 2 (October)
18. Black Panther: Wakanda Forever (November)
19. The Flash (November)
20. Babylon (December)
21. Aquaman and the Lost Kingdom (December)
22. Avatar 2 (December)

22 Prophetic Dates of the Year

1. Sunday, January 2, 2022
2. Monday, January 17, 2022
3. Wednesday, February 2, 2022
4. Thursday, February 24, 2022
5. Tuesday, March 8, 2022
6. Wednesday, March 30, 2022
7. Saturday, April 9, 2022
8. Friday, April 29, 2022
9. Sunday, May 8, 2022
10. Saturday, May 28, 2022
11. Wednesday, June 15, 2022
12. Thursday, June 30, 2022
13. Monday, July 4, 2022
14. Saturday, July 30, 2022
15. Tuesday, August 9, 2022
16. Saturday, August 20, 2022
17. Sunday, September 11, 2022
18. Saturday, October 8, 2022
19. Monday, October 31, 2022
20. Friday, November 11, 2022
21. Friday, November 25, 2022
22. Wednesday, December 21, 2022

22 People to Watch in 2022

1. Taylor Swift, Singer
2. Luka Doncic, NBA Superstar
3. Guy Fieri, Chef
4. Roman Reigns, Wrestler
5. Kamala Harris, Vice President
6. Patrick Mahomes II, Football Player
7. Daniel Craig, Actor
8. James Corden, Talk Show Host
9. Dua Lipa, Singer
10. Nick Saban Jr., Alabama Football Coach
11. Reese Witherspoon, Actress
12. Elon Musk, Entrepreneur
13. Lil Nas X, Rapper
14. Ted Cruz, Politician
15. Channing Tatum, Actor
16. Ryan Seacrest, Radio & TV Personality
17. Lebron James, Basketball Player
18. Chuck Schumer, Senator
19. Joe Biden, President
20. Fernando Tatis Jr, Baseball Player
21. Jay-Z, Rapper
22. Michael B. Jordan, Actor

CHAPTER 2
Fun Facts for Twenty-Two

Entertainment
- Taylor Swift wrote a song entitled "22".
- The Paramount Pictures Logo has 22 stars.
- Jay-Z has a song "22 Twos." He rhymes the words, "too," "to," and "two" 22 times in the first verse.
- In *The Avengers*, there is a London bus that has 22 on it. It is an actual bus route in London.
- *22 Jump Street* was a comedy film made in 2014 which is about two undercover officers learning to become adults and work together to solve a case.
- *22 July* is a dramatic real-life movie from 2018 depicting Norway's deadliest terror attack where 77 teens were murdered at a youth camp in 2011
- The game show *Deal or No Deal*, made famous in the UK, had 22 boxes to choose from.
- "22 Acacia Avenue" is a song by Iron Maiden on the album, *The Number of the Beast.*
- *Revista 22* is a magazine published in Romania.
- On February 10, 1961, an episode of The *Twilight Zone* tv series was entitled "Twenty-Two". It is the episode about a hospitalized

dancer who has nightmares and an evil nurse inviting her to Room 22 which was the hospital's morgue.
- Buddy Holly, who was a singer, died at the age of 22.

Sports
- The 22nd Summer Olympics were held in 1980 in Russia.
- Soccer has 22 players on a field at the same time.
- In the NFL, there are always 22 players on the field.
- Emmit Smith wore #22 on his jersey and was inducted into the NFL Hall of Fame in 2010.
- In the sport of Cricket, the length of a pitch is 22 yards.
- Professional Players that wore #22 Jersey:
  - Rickey Henderson, MLB
  - Clyde Drexler, NBA
  - Clayton Kershaw, MLB
  - Moses Malone, NBA
  - Elgin Baylor, NBA
  - Mike Schmidt, MLB
  - Roger Clemens, MLB
  - Brett Hull, NHL

Historical

- John F. Kennedy was assassinated on November 22, 1963.
- Alabama is the 22nd State to be inducted into the Union.
- The 22nd Amendment was passed in 1947 limiting Presidents to two four-year terms.
- The Titanic traveled at a speed of 22 knots before crashing into an iceberg.
- Grover Cleveland was the 22nd President of the United States. He was the first Democrat elected after the Civil War in 1885. He was also the only President to leave the White House and return for a second term four years later.

General

- Superextraordinarisimo has 22 letters and is the largest word in the Spanish language. It means extraordinary.
- A million dollars in $100 bills weighs around 22 pounds.
- 22 degrees Celsius is 71.6 Fahrenheit.
- In Bingo, 22 is referred to as "two little ducks".
- The BBC or British Broadcasting Company was founded in 1922.
- There is a .22 caliber rifle.
- A regulation shuffleboard table is 22 feet in length.

- "Catch 22" means dilemma or quandary.
- 22 is atomic number for titanium.
- The F-22 Raptor is also known as the stealth fighter aircraft in the United States Airforce.
- In France, "22" is a warning that the police are on the way.
- The Roman numeral for 22 is XXII.
- A woman that is 22 weeks pregnant is in her fifth month of pregnancy and the baby is the size of a coconut.
- SR 22 is a state highway in California that runs for 14.725 miles.
- The United Nations has declared 2022 as the International Year of Glass.
- The Hebrew alphabet has 22 letters.
- The average distance from the Earth to the moon is 238,900 miles, 2+3+8+9 = 22.

Biblical
- The Book of Revelation has 22 chapters
- Jair, one of the judges of Israel, served for 22 years.
- Jeroboam was the first king of the divided Israel in the Northern Kingdom. He reigned 22 years (930 to 909 BC).
- There are 22 generations from Adam to Jacob.
- Ahab who was the worst king of Israel reigned for 22 years (874-853 BC).

- King Amon, who ruled for only two years over Judah, began his reign at 22 years old. He was one of the worst kings to rule over Judah.
- Ahaziah was 22 when he became king. He reigned one year and did evil in the eyes of God, 2 Chronicles 22:2-4.
- Jesus quoted from Psalm 22:1 when He was on the Cross.
- God created 22 things during creation.
- When Moses raised up the tabernacle of God, there were 22,000 Levites consecrated to serve.
- 3 John chronologically is the 22nd book of the New Testament.
- The word "mystery" is mentioned 22 times in the KJV Bible and only in the New Testament.
- There are 22 books of the Bible that have 22 chapters.
- Psalm 25 has 22 verses and is about God removing shame.
- There are 58 chapters in the Bible that have 22 verses:
  - Genesis 6
  - Genesis 8
  - Genesis 28
  - Genesis 48
  - Exodus 1
  - Exodus 3
  - Exodus 13

- Numbers 19
- Deuteronomy 10
- Deuteronomy 16
- Deuteronomy 18
- Deuteronomy 24
- Ruth 1
- Ruth 4
- 1 Samuel 4
- 1 Samuel 8
- 1 Samuel 24
- 2 Samuel 21
- 2 Chronicles 4
- 2 Chronicles 7
- 2 Chronicles 13
- Ezra 6
- Esther 1
- Job 1
- Job 8
- Job 10
- Job 14
- Job 16
- Job 32
- Psalm 25
- Psalm 33
- Psalm 34
- Psalm 38
- Psalm 103
- Proverbs 2
- Ecclesiastes 3
- Isaiah 2
- Isaiah 8

- Isaiah 13
- Isaiah 36
- Isaiah 38
- Isaiah 48
- Isaiah 60
- Jeremiah 8
- Jeremiah 14
- Jeremiah 27
- Jeremiah 34
- Jeremiah 42
- Lamentations 1
- Lamentations 2
- Lamentations 4
- Lamentations 5
- Ezekiel 10
- Ephesians 2
- 2 Timothy 4
- 1 Peter 3
- 2 Peter 2
- Revelation 3

As you go through this year, you will see why all of these little nuggets are important to helping you understand what is happening in 2022. Be consciously aware to look for these things in your daily life knowing God can confirm His message and reveal His truth through the simplest of things.

CHAPTER 3
2022 Vision

The main reason for authoring this book is to give us vision and direction from God concerning this upcoming year. Proverbs 29:18 says, *"without a vision the people perish."* When I speak of vision, I am referring to having a purpose in life and establishing a plan to live by that helps us to be prosperous. As Christians, we find our purpose as we are connected to God and seek to discover His will for our lives through the scriptures. There are many ways to find our purpose in life or the purpose for a specific year. The Lord has given me special insight to understand the different numbers mentioned in the Bible to give revelation on what to expect from Him in a particular year. This year the number 22 is the number to dissect to release the vision for 2022. My goal is to teach you what you can expect from God and what God expects of you in the coming year. If there is no vision, there cannot be any direction. If there is no direction, you will wander around aimlessly without any purpose for the 365 days of 2022 that are ahead. This vision may not be the most glamorous insight you want to hear, but it will bring revelation of the will of God for your life in 2022 that is based on the meaning of 22 when it is mentioned in the Bible. This is what you need to hear and what God wants you to focus in on in 2022 to be successful.

Three-Fold Vision For 2022

MARRIAGE

Marriage is mentioned 22 times in the Bible. In Genesis 2:22, we read that God brought forth a woman from the rib of a man to be by his side. Marriage is the first institution or organization created by God, and it is for men and women to live together as one. God created marriage for four main reasons:

- To be a cure for loneliness

    "And the Lord God said, It is not good that the man should be alone; I will make him an help meet for him." *Genesis 2:18*

    Marriage provides a means for companionship and connection. We are not created to be alone or to be by ourselves. Marriage provides a life partner to share the burdens and blessings of life through our journey in life.

- To be a way to become more productive

    "Two are better than one; because they have a good reward for their labour." *Ecclesiastes 4:9*

The Bible teaches us that two are better than one and that we can have a greater impact together than on our own. Marriage should make us more fruitful in our life endeavors.

- To be a means to reproduce and populate the earth

"So God created man in his own image, in the image of God created he him; male and female created he them. And God blessed them, and God said unto them, Be fruitful, and multiply, and replenish the earth, and subdue it: and have dominion over the fish of the sea, and over the fowl of the air, and over every living thing that moveth upon the earth." Genesis 1:27-28

God designed marriage as a way to start and develop a family.

- To be a visual example to others of God's love for us

"Husbands, love your wives, even as Christ also loved the church, and gave himself for it; That he might sanctify and cleanse it with the washing of water by the word, That he might present it to

himself a glorious church, not having spot, or wrinkle, or any such thing; but that it should be holy and without blemish. So ought men to love their wives as their own bodies. He that loveth his wife loveth himself. For no man ever yet hated his own flesh; but nourisheth and cherisheth it, even as the Lord the church: For we are members of his body, of his flesh, and of his bones. For this cause shall a man leave his father and mother, and shall be joined unto his wife, and they two shall be one flesh. This is a great mystery: but I speak concerning Christ and the church. Nevertheless let every one of you in particular so love his wife even as himself; and the wife see that she reverence her husband." Ephesians 5:25-33

Marriage is a way to witness to others about the love of God by expressing our love for one another.

Although marriage is a gift from God to mankind, many have failed as the divorce rate continues to rise, not just in the world, but in the church. Marriages are failing because of the selfishness of mankind and our rebellious desire to have our own way. Today's society contradicts the basic principles of the Word of God. We are told not to yield to one another and never compromise. We have been lied to by thinking marriage is about happiness when really, it is about holiness.

Top Reasons Marriages Fail

- The marriage was all about the wedding
- Lack of respect
- Unfair fighting
- Not speaking your spouse's love language
- The internet
- Selfishness
- Unequally yoked
- Lack of counsel
- No sexual intimacy
- Unfaithfulness
- No dating after "I Do"
- Immaturity
- Lack of prioritizing
- Unforgiveness
- Lack of liking your spouse

I could go on and on ...

Marriage is a heavenly covenant that is eternal, not an earthly contract that can be broken when things get tough in the relationship. This is a year God wants us to renew our commitment to our marriages and allow Him to root out everything that is hindering us from having successful relationships. The problem is usually found in us and not in our spouses. Allow God to do a new thing in your marriage in 2022.

DOUBLE DISORDER

2022 will not be a normal year, as the number 22 is made up of 11x2 which equals 22. Eleven is a number of chaos and confusion, so 22 is a doubling of disorder. The book of Revelation has 22 chapters and is mostly about the trouble that occurs during the last days before Jesus' return. King Ahab reigned for 22 years and was the worst king of Israel who promoted evil throughput the land. King Amon started his reigned at the age of 22 and was the worst king of Judah.

Disorder is defined as, "disturbing the regular order of something." It is an abnormal confusion that creates havoc. With everything we have gone through in the world over the last few years, the last thing we want to hear is that not only will things get worse, but that there will be a doubling of the trouble. Disorder is never from God. It is always from the devil.

"For God is not the author of confusion, but of peace, as in all churches of the saints." 1 Corinthians 14:33a

Mental disorder, physical disorder, personality disorder, financial disorder, and civil disorder will all occur at a disturbing level in 2022. Disorder happens in three ways:

1. Sin
2. Life circumstances
3. Inheritance

- **Sin**

   Believe it or not, because disorder is from the devil, we must understand we open the door to disorder through sin. When we willfully disobey God's instruction in scripture, it creates an opening for the devil to get in and bring confusion.

   "He that diggeth a pit shall fall into it; and whoso breaketh an hedge, a serpent shall bite him." Ecclesiastes 10:8

- **Life Circumstances**

   Life circumstances are negative events that directly impact the mental, physical, emotional, financial, and spiritual health of an individual. They could be devastating events that happened as a child or great losses you experienced as an adult that want to define you and steal your hope for a better future.

"These things I have spoken unto you, that in me ye might have peace. In the world ye shall have tribulation: but be of good cheer; I have overcome the world." John 16:33

- **Inheritance**
  Generational curses, or family spirits, can be passed down from one generation to the next and continue to create disorder in your entire family lineage.

"Thou shalt not bow down thyself to them, nor serve them: for I the Lord thy God am a jealous God, visiting the iniquity of the fathers upon the children unto the third and fourth generation of them that hate me;" Exodus 20:5

In whatever way disorder has entered your life or become a part of our society, there is only one real cure ... Jesus!!!

In the midst of all the disorder that will happen in our lives and in our world, know this - Jesus is our only hope!!!

How to Maintain Order in Chaos

1. Trust the Lord, Proverbs 3:4-5
2. Resist the devil, James 4:7
3. Pray for a sound mind, 2 Timothy 1:7
4. Break all generation curses, Luke 10:19
5. Feed your spirit, John 6:51
   Whatever you feed will grow; whatever you starve will die!
6. Do good, Titus 3:8
7. Meditate on the Word, Joshua 1:8
8. Connect with godly people, 1 Corinthians 15:33
9. Prioritize, Matthew 6:33
10. Think positive, Philippians 4:8

Actively engage and apply these truths to reduce the confusion that 2022 will certainly bring into our world.

HOLY SPIRIT

The scripture of the year is John 20:22, where Jesus breathed on His disciples and said, *"Receive ye the Holy Spirit."* With everything going on, we will definitely need a dose of the Holy Ghost to vaccinate us from discouragement. The Holy Spirit has six main jobs to perform in 2022:

1. The Holy Spirit *Instructs*

    "Which things also we speak, not in the words which man's wisdom teacheth, but which the Holy Ghost teacheth; comparing spiritual things with spiritual." 1 Corinthians 2:13

2. The Holy Spirit *Reminds*

    "But the Comforter, which is the Holy Ghost, whom the Father will send in my name, he shall teach you all things, and bring all things to your remembrance, whatsoever I have said unto you." John 14:26

3. The Holy Spirit *Guides*

    Howbeit when he, the Spirit of truth, is come, he will guide you into all truth: for he shall not speak of himself; but whatsoever he shall hear, that shall he speak: and he will shew you things to come." John 16:13

4. The Holy Spirit *Declares*

"Howbeit when he, the Spirit of truth, is come, he will guide you into all truth: for he shall not speak of himself; but whatsoever he shall hear, that shall he speak: and he will shew you things to come. He shall glorify me: for he shall receive of mine, and shall shew it unto you. All things that the Father hath are mine: therefore said I, that he shall take of mine, and shall shew it unto you." John 16:13-15

5. The Holy Spirit *Reveals*

"But God hath revealed them unto us by his Spirit: for the Spirit searcheth all things, yea, the deep things of God." 1 Corinthians 2:10

6. The Holy Spirit *Comforts*

"And I will pray the Father, and he shall give you another Comforter, that he may abide with you for ever;" John 14:16

A Spirit-less person is a life-less person. In Genesis 2:7, Adam was given life but did not become a living soul until God breathed into his nostrils. We need God to breathe on us this year, so we can be alive and not just live. In order to do that, we must follow six simple instructions for 2022.

Holy Spirit Guidelines For 2022

1. Live in the Spirit, Galatians 5:25
2. Walk in the Spirit, Galatians 5:16
3. Give in the Spirit, 2 Corinthians 8:3-5
4. Pray in the Spirit, Ephesians 6:18
5. Worship in the Spirit, Philippians 3:3
6. Love in the Spirit, Colossians 1:8
7. Forgive in the Spirit, Colossians 3:13

This is going to be a tough year in many ways, but you can make it with the help of the Holy Spirit. Just cooperate with God, and you will succeed in 2022.

CHAPTER 4
Old Testament Speak to Me

Genesis 22

This chapter contains one of the greatest stories in the entire Bible. Abraham is tested by God to prove his love for the Lord by sacrificing his only son Isaac. It is a story of how Abraham was willing to yield to and obey God regardless of what was asked of him. In the end, God honored Abraham's loyalty and faithfulness by providing a ram as a substitute sacrifice for his son. This will be a challenging year in many ways, and it might become more difficult if God decides to test our commitment to Him. Testing is one thing God uses to prove what is genuinely in our hearts. It is important to pass every test in 2022 to prove to God our internal commitment to Him.

There Are Three Main Reasons
Why God Tests Us:

1. To prove our love for God, Deuteronomy 8:2
2. To produce fruit, James 1:2-3
3. To provide an avenue for blessing, James 1:12

Life is not always fair, and it is never easy. Testing is a way to measure our motives. But, being tested in life is an invitation to win. No matter what God allows in 2022, be determined to pass the test, and win the race.

TESTING OUR FAITH IN 2022

Exodus 22

God is making it noticeably clear to Moses that when we are Christians living in a sinful world, we have a social responsibility to maintain a godly moral standard.

What is Our Social Responsibility?
1. Do not steal from others, v. 1-2
2. Make restitution when you are wrong, v. 3-4
3. Do not give something away that you would not want to keep for yourself, v. 10-11
4. Do not make commitments you cannot keep, v. 15-17
5. Reject all witchcraft, v. 18
6. Do not commit sexual sins, v. 19
7. Never mistreat strangers, v. 21
8. Do not take advantage of widows or orphans, v. 22

9. Do not lend or borrow money, v. 25-27
10. Do not curse your leaders, v. 28
11. Pay tithe on every increase, v. 29-30
12. Eat healthy, v. 31

To say there is a lot to chew on there is a massive understatement. We have a social responsibility to do the right thing as Christians living in this world. You honor God when you fulfill your social responsibility to mankind. Be a witness to others, not by preaching the Gospel, but by living out the truth in your daily life.

FULFILL YOUR SOCIAL
RESPONSIBILITY IN 2022

Leviticus 22

The Lord is speaking through Moses to the priests regarding their reverence to the Lord. God is reminding the leaders to make sure there is a separation between the average person and the priest. All priests had to adhere to certain rules to be qualified to lead the people.

Five Rules for Priests

1. Take ministry responsibilities seriously, v. 1-13
2. Nightly baths or showers, v. 6
3. No unhealthy eating habits, v. 14
4. To oversee the animals offered for sacrifice were without blemish or defect, v. 16-25
5. Live holy lives since God is holy, v. 31-33

It is important to the Lord to have leaders who have holy hands and humbled hearts. We are disqualified to lead others when we cannot control our own fleshly desires. We as believers in the New Testament are all considered priests in the eyes of the Lord.

> *"But ye are a chosen generation, a royal priesthood, an holy nation, a peculiar people; that ye should shew forth the praises of him who hath called you out of darkness into his marvellous light;"*
> *1 Peter 2:9*

As priests and leaders, we need to uphold the standards of God. God does not want a lack of integrity in the pulpit. He wants us to lead by example.

FOLLOW PRIESTLY GUIDELINES IN 2022

Numbers 22

This is a remarkable story of how God uses a donkey to save Balaam's life. Balak, a Moabite King, is worried the Israelites were going to destroy their land using military force. Balak sends a message to Balaam that he is willing to pay Balaam to curse Israel to save his land. As Balaam is headed to meet with the king, a problem arises. The donkey sees an angel in the road trying to prevent their progress toward Moab. The donkey sees the angel, but Balaam does not. The donkey sees the angel standing in the road with a huge sword and attempts to go around the angel, but the angel moves to get in front of Balaam's donkey again. The donkey does not know what else to do, so it lays down in the street. Balaam gets aggravated and hits the donkey. Then the donkey speaks and says, "Why are you hitting me?" It was then that Balaam saw the angel of the Lord who was trying to stop him from going to Moab and cursing Israel. This year we must have better discernment and better listening skills. There is something wrong if an animal is hearing from God and we are not. It is simple - listen more and talk less in 2022. Ask God for discernment to know His Word and for courage to obey His will.

BE SMARTER THAN A
DONKEY IN 2022

Deuteronomy 22

This chapter is about honoring your marriage vows and respecting your spouse. These rules seem simple, but they are important to follow if we are going to have successful marriages.

Seven Rules for Successful Marriages

1. Pay attention to your spouse, v. 1-4
2. Let women be feminine and men be masculine, v. 5
3. Walk in agreement and unity, v. 8-10
4. Stay sexually pure, v. 13-18
5. Never bring up the "divorce" word, v. 19
6. Never commit adultery, v. 22
7. Never force your will upon your spouse, v. 28

These are great truths to follow in every marriage. To the degree you follow these instructions is to the degree you will be successful as a couple. These rules help us to honor our spouse and to honor God.

HONOR YOUR MARRIAGE IN 2022

Joshua 22

The children of Israel were ready to go to war against their own people over a misunderstanding. Joshua felt like there were some people who were being rebellious and abandoning godly principles. Joshua sent a group of people to talk with some of the children of Israel, to seek a resolution before going to war. Fortunately, they were able to reach an understanding and have reconciliation. This chapter is a great lesson on how to reach a peaceful resolution instead of going to war.

Five Lessons to Learn to Avoid War

1. Seek to understand, not be understood
2. Never make a decision when you are angry
3. Ask, never assume
4. Walk in love
5. Do not rush to judgement

Christians need to seek peace not war.

> *"Let us therefore follow after the things which make for peace, and things wherewith one may edify another."*
> *Romans 14:19*

There will be many opportunities for us to act inappropriately and go to war in 2022. Stay humble, and chase peace. Forgive and seek reconciliation in 2022.

SEEK PEACEFUL RESOLUTIONS IN 2022

1 Samuel 22

This is a wonderful story about David and how he left Gath and went to Adullam. He was on the run and fleeing from those who were trying to kill him. He went into hiding by going to a place of refuge in a cave in Adullam. He could not go to his house, or the palace, or even the church to get away and be with the Lord. So, he sought the only place he thought he could go to. The cave was his closet. Unfortunately, the Bible says 400 men found him who were worse off than David!

They were:
- In distress = desperate
- In debt = broke
- In discontent = depressed

It was here in the cave of Adullam running for his life from Saul, that David learned how to help others when he was hurting himself.

"Look not every man on his own things, but every man also on the things of others." Philippians 2:4

It is hard to help others when you are hurting yourself, but it can be done if you turn your heart towards God and remember to put others above yourself. David wrote Psalm 57 while he was in the cave. This Psalm reveals four things about David's true heart.

What Kind of Heart did David Have?

1. Humble and merciful heart, v. 1
2. Prayerful heart, v. 2
3. Realistic and honest heart, v. 4,6
4. Trusting heart, v. 9,11

David's heart was right with God because he was a man after God's own heart. When you have the heart of God, you can help others when you are hurting yourself.

HAVE THE HEART OF GOD IN 2022

2 Samuel 22

David had many talents including being a skilled musician and a talented songwriter. He played in front of great crowds and played for a crowd of one in front of Saul. David wrote more Psalms or songs than anyone else. Singing, playing, and writing songs were an important part of his life. This chapter reveals a very long song of David that contained several essential elements that every godly song must include to honor God.

Five Elements of Godly Songs

1. Songs that refer to God's power
2. Songs that are doctrinally sound
3. Songs that show our vulnerability
4. Songs that speak life
5. Songs that touch the heart of God

David not only wrote the songs, but he also played the songs and sung the songs. Worship was a way David used to connect with God. You may not be a song writer or singer, but I want to challenge you to step out of your box and write a song to the Lord. Just get a piece of paper and express your feelings to God. It may not rhyme or be sung in church, but it is your song to the Lord. Your song can be a Psalm or even a letter, but go take time, and write your thoughts down on paper to God.

WRITE YOUR SONG IN 2022

1 Kings 22

The book of 1 Kings begins with a nation united under David's leadership and ends as a divided kingdom with the death of Ahab who was a wicked king.

What Happened?
- People turned on their godly leaders
- People did not acknowledge God as the ultimate king
- People appointed leaders who ignored God
- People compromised their beliefs and conformed to the evil ways of their leaders
- People accepted the unacceptable
- People trusted in the lies of the false prophets

As people tolerated occasional wrongdoing, it turned into blatant wickedness that led to the nation being ruined. This is a great story that teaches us a great lesson. We must put God first in all things, and make sure when our leaders talk, that it lines up with the Word of God. Even the godly prophet Micaiah initially fell into the trap of agreeing with the 400 false prophets to tell the king what he wanted to hear. Ultimately, he spoke the truth and did the right thing, but you always have to speak the truth regardless of consequences.

SPEAK THE TRUTH IN 2022

2 Kings 22

It was extremely rare to find a king who completely obeyed God. Josiah was the best King of Judah, and he began his reign as a child at age eight.

What did Josiah do to Make Himself a Great King?

- He sought the will of the Lord
- He purged Judah of idols and false worship
- He repaired the damaged temple
- He renewed the people's covenant with God
- He encouraged righteousness in Judah
- He stood up against sin and evil

Josiah's zeal and passion for God ought to remind us to start early when it comes to teaching our kids the principles of God. Our children and youth are our future. Children's ministry within a church is not an opportunity for some untrained adult to babysit our kids. If our kids are important, let us prove it by teaching and training them now. Let us invest in them today, so we can reap a harvest from them tomorrow.

"Train up a child in the way he should go: and when he is old, he will not depart from it." Proverbs 22:6

Let us raise our children correctly by teaching and training them in the things of God at an early age.

TRAIN THE CHILDREN IN 2022

1 Chronicles 22

Out of David's horrible mistake comes something good. Israel purchases land that would become the site of God's Temple. The temple would be a place people would go to worship God and be reminded that God can take tragedy and turn it into triumph. The one bad thing about beginning to build the temple was that David would only be the overseer. That task would fall to his son Solomon. Solomon was young and inexperienced, so David passed on some knowledge and even asked other wise people to help his son. One of the most important jobs in building the temple was to make sure there were enough watchman to guard and protect the temple from being attacked. In fact, being a watchman was the first job that God gave to mankind.

"And the Lord God took the man, and put him into the garden of Eden to dress it and to keep it." Genesis 2:15

Watchman were bodyguards and doorkeepers that protected and preserved the things of God. We watch because, according to 2 Corinthians 2:11, Satan can gain an advantage over us when we are ignorant of his devices. Throughout scripture we are encouraged to watch over things to keep what God creates.

Seven Things to Watch Over

1. Our brothers and sisters, Genesis 4:9
2. Our homes, Ecclesiastes 12:3
3. Our churches, Psalm 127:1
4. Our mouths, Psalm 141:3
5. Our respect towards God, Habakkuk 2:20
6. Our obedience, John 14:15
7. Our faith, 2 Timothy 4:7

God was turning things around for Israel, but they had to learn it was their responsibility to keep whatever God creates.

BE A WATCHMAN IN 2022

2 Chronicles 22

Ahaziah was appointed king by the people of Jerusalem, but he only reigned for one year and was considered evil in all his ways. Part of the reason he was so evil was that he received so much bad advice. He had counselors around him who led him in the wrong direction. Even his mother gave him evil instructions. Getting bad counsel and following the wrong advice will lead to destruction.

> *"He that walketh with wise men shall be wise: but a companion of fools shall be destroyed." Proverbs 13:20*

> *"Without counsel purposes are disappointed: but in the multitude of counsellors they are established." Proverbs 15:22*

Basically, Ahaziah failed because he got the wrong counsel and advice. It is extremely important that we seek wise counsel from wise counselors. Our success is often determined by the company we keep and the advice we apply to our lives.

What is Godly Counsel?

1. Godly counsel is always given after prayerful consideration.
2. Godly counsel always is given in love and leads to love.
3. Godly counsel always comes from Godly counselors.
4. Godly counsel always agrees with scripture.
5. Godly counsel always reveals blinds spots.
6. Godly counsel always stretches us to grow.

If you are seeking counsel, then seek advice from someone who knows what they are talking about and lives a life of integrity. You will need all the godly counsel you can get to make it through this year, so make sure you are getting it through the correct sources.

LISTEN ONLY TO GODLY ADVICE IN 2022

Job 22

Job 22 is like a bad movie sequel. The speeches of Job's so-called friends continue. This is Eliphaz's third and final speech to Job. He really says nothing new to Job other than being a little more specific concerning Job's sins. The fact of the matter is not only is Eliphaz guessing, but he is wrong. He just cannot shake the heresy that Job is suffering because it is God's judgment for his evil deeds. Eliphaz actually states some truths about repentance and forgiveness.

Some Truths from Eliphaz

1. A sinner's view of God is small, v. 12
2. Sinners take sinning too lightly, v. 14
3. Sin leads to more sin, v. 15
4. Sinners need to ask for forgiveness, v. 21-22
5. Sinners who repent will be restored, v. 23-30

These are awesome truths for sinners, but Job was not one of them. Job had to sit there and listen to another speech given to him by the stubborn, Eliphaz. Stubbornness convinces us that we are right, and others are wrong. Stubborn people are unreasonable people who are difficult to manage because they are adamant about their wrong beliefs. Avoid being a stubborn know-it-all kind of person in 2022 and allow the humility of the Lord to control your life.

REJECT STUBBORNNESS IN 2022

Psalm 22

Psalm 22 is a song of David about someone crying out to God in agony and thanking God for rescuing them. It is a Psalm that links the Old Testament with the story of Jesus' crucifixion. Jesus even quoted verse one while He suffered on the Cross. This Psalm is called the "Psalm of the Cross." All of us can identify with suffering and pain. We all have felt abandoned in our moments of greatest need. We have questioned the Lord and have asked questions like:

- What is going on?
- Where is God?
- Why me?

Not only does this Psalm contain the agony of defeat but also the thrill of victory. We need to remember two great truths from this Psalm when we are going through tough times.

Two Great Truths

1. God hears our cry, v. 1-21

   God hears us when we pray even when it feels He is ignoring us.

2. God heals our hurts, v. 22-31

   God always heals our hurts even when it feels like He is slow to respond.

   One of the hardest things to do in life as a Christian is to learn how to carry our cross and to trust the Lord that everything will work out for our good.

CARRY YOUR CROSS IN 2022

Proverbs 22

Each chapter in Proverbs provides us with a ton of sermon sentences designed to provide practical wisdom. Proverbs 22 is like a New Year's Commitment list, giving us things to work on and apply to our lives throughout 2022 to be successful.

22 New Year's Commitments

1. Build character, v. 1
2. Love everyone, v. 2
3. Run from evil, v. 3
4. Walk in humility, v. 4
5. Control your soul, v. 5
6. Train your children, v. 6
7. Never borrow from others, v. 7
8. Sow generously, v. 8
9. Give to the poor, v. 9, 16
10. Remove yourself from strife, v. 10
11. Pursue pureness, v. 11
12. Get knowledge from God's Word, v. 12
13. Not be lazy, v. 13
14. Not be seduced, v. 14
15. Correct children correctly, v. 15
16. Seek wisdom from the wise, v. 17-20
17. Not sue others, v. 22-23
18. Stay away from angry people, v. 24
19. Transfer good to others, v. 25
20. Never co-sign for another's debt, v. 26-27
21. Set boundaries, v. 28
22. Improve your skills, v. 29

Great Proverb; Great truths! Use these 22 commitments to better yourself in 2022.

COMMIT TO BETTER YOURSELF IN 2022

Isaiah 22

The prophet Isaiah warned God's people, but they refused to listen. Israel decided against trusting the Lord and used every means available to mankind to protect themselves. Their education could not save them, their weapons could not save them, even their neighbors could not save them from the attack of their enemies. Israel rejected Isaiah's prophecy to return to the Lord, so they were destroyed. Isaiah was hurt and angry by their punishment. He wanted only the best for Israel, but unfortunately, he wanted better for them than they wanted for themselves. Trusting God means letting go and letting God take over our lives. All of our human effort cannot save us if we are trusting in ourselves. We need God to guide and lead the way. Israel did everything they could to prepare for war. They stored up water, inspected the walls, had watchman ready, and their weapons were working, but they never asked God for help. This is a sad story of a group of people who thought they knew better than God. When you are faced with trouble, you have to turn to God for help.

> *"For this people's heart is waxed gross, and their ears are dull of hearing, and their eyes they have closed; lest at any time they should see with their eyes and hear with their ears, and should understand with their heart, and should be converted, and I should heal them."*
> *Matthew 13:15*

> *"Look unto me, and be ye saved, all the ends of the earth: for I am God, and there is none else."* *Isaiah 45:22*

> *"Casting all your care upon him; for he careth for you."* *1 Peter 5:7*

Only God can save you as you put your trust in Him.

TRUST GOD, NOT MAN IN 2022

Jeremiah 22

God is warning the leaders, through the prophet Jeremiah, that judgment will come if they do not turn from their evil ways.

Seven Sins of Leaders

1. Oppressed others
2. Violence
3. Murder
4. Mistreated the widows
5. Stole from people
6. Hard-headed
7. Hard-hearted

God warns them that judgment will come if change does not happen soon. Jeremiah calls on them to repent and says unless they do repent, God will show no mercy. The important thing to remember about this chapter is that even though the leaders were evil and were so angry, the Lord still showed mercy by expressing to them that they still had time to change. It is encouraging to remind ourselves that God has extreme patience with His people. God loves us and wants us to be saved.

"For the Son of man is come to seek and to save that which was lost." Luke 19:10

"Who will have all men to be saved, and to come unto the knowledge of the truth."
1 Timothy 2:4

There is still time to change and make things right with God.

STILL TIME TO CHANGE IN 2022

Ezekiel 22

Jerusalem had become a city of violence where crime and evil was running rampant. People had no respect for spiritual things; they would take advantage of the poor, and the family unit had become unimportant. Sexual immorality was at an all-time high, and the moral decline entered the judicial system as the judges were being bribed. All of this happened because the people turned away from God, and the leaders held no one accountable for their sins. Countries, cities, and individuals cannot despise God without experiencing consequences from the Lord.

"For the wages of sin is death; but the gift of God is eternal life through Jesus Christ our Lord." Romans 6:23

The evil was not just taking place among sinners in the world, but among the believers in the church as well. The preachers and prophets were sugar-coating the truth and whitewashing the Word. That is part of the problem we have in our world today. We have too many weak-kneed, limp-wristed, wimpy preachers who are petting people's devils instead of casting them out. In the midst of all the reported wickedness and impending judgment, there is one of my favorite verses in the Bible found in Ezekiel 22:30,

> *"And I sought for a man among them, that should make up the hedge, and stand in the gap before me for the land, that I should not destroy it: but I found none."*

God sought out a man to stand in the gap, stand up for God, and speak the truth. The sad news is He could not find one. The Bible says, *"God found none."* My question for you in 2022 is, "Can there be someone found today who will stand up for God and speak the truth?" I say, "yes," and I say, let it be you and me.

STAND UP AND SPEAK OUT FOR GOD IN 2022

CHAPTER 5
New Testament Speak to Me

Matthew 22

This chapter is filled with insincere questions from the Pharisees and the Sadducees to Jesus. They questioned Him, not to gain wisdom or understanding, but in an attempt to trick Jesus into answering incorrectly. Despite all the questioning the chapter begins with, what I want to emphasize the most is … The Wedding Feast. This is a parable which means it is an earthly story with a heavenly meaning. Parables may be illustrations or actual stories that took place, but either way, there is a message to be learned. A king was having a wedding festival for his son and invited certain people to attend. All of them refused which made the king so angry that he sent his army out to burn the city. The king then sent his servants out to give an open invitation to anyone that wanted to come to the wedding feast. Everyone was invited to come, whether they were considered good or bad. The place was filled with people from all over, who were invited to come celebrate the king's son's wedding. Now in those days, it was a custom for the wedding guests to be issued special garments to wear at the banquet. It was an insult and offensive to the host not to wear the garments that were provided to the guests. However, one guest did not wear the special clothing and was bound and kicked out of the party. The clothes were a picture of the righteousness of God that must be worn for us to enter the Kingdom of God.

> *"I will greatly rejoice in the Lord, my soul shall be joyful in my God; for he hath clothed me with the garments of salvation, he hath covered me with the robe of righteousness, as a bridegroom decketh himself with ornaments, and as a bride adorneth herself with her jewels." Isaiah 61:10*

There is an open invitation for everyone to come to the Lord regardless of who you are, where you came from, or what you have done. However, you must be willing to put on God's robe of righteousness, seek forgiveness for your sins, turn from your evil ways, and begin to serve the Lord. You cannot reject the offer of God and expect to live a good life.

AN OPEN INVITATION TO COME TO JESUS IN 2022

Luke 22

Luke 22 is a long chapter with a lot going on. We read of Jesus' final hours before the crucifixion on the cross.

11 Events in Jesus' Final Hours

1. It was Passover season, v. 1
2. Chief Priests and Scribes were plotting to kill Jesus, v. 2
3. Satan entered Judas, v. 3
4. Last Supper with Disciples, v. 7-16
5. Communion instituted, v. 17-20
6. Jesus called out His betrayer, v. 21-23
7. Peter denied Christ, v. 31-34, 54-65
8. Jesus agonized in the Garden of Gethsemane, v. 39-44
9. Disciples fell asleep on Jesus, v. 45-46
10. Jesus was arrested on false charges, v. 47-53
11. Jesus stood before Pontius Pilate, v. 66-71

All of these events took place on Thursday of Holy Week in Jesus' final hours on Earth. The Thursday of Holy Week is known as "Maundy Thursday" or "Mandate Thursday." Jesus gave a mandate to us for us to serve and love one another. However, the constant theme of Luke 22 is betrayal.

Judas betrayed Him. Peter betrayed Him. The religious leaders betrayed Him. As Jesus was winding down His final hours here on Earth, His closest friends betrayed Him. As we are definitely living in the last of the last days, let us be prepared for possible betrayal by guarding our hearts and protecting our souls. Betrayal is unfortunately inevitable, and if it happened to Jesus, it could happen to us. Remember, we cannot control others, but we can control ourselves. We cannot keep others from betraying us, but we can commit not to backstab or betray others.

GUARD AGAINST BETRAYAL IN 2022

Acts 22

Paul is speaking to a crowd of people and begins by giving them a resume of who he is. He tells them where he is from, who he knows, and what he has gone through up to this point. He is giving them his testimony and is encouraging them to repent and be baptized. Paul's desire was for all mankind everywhere to be introduced to Jesus Christ and be saved. Paul understood that you could be saved without water-baptism, but you should want to be water-baptized if you are saved.

Principles of Water-Baptism

1. Water-baptism is subsequent (after) salvation
2. Water-baptism signifies ownership
3. Water-baptism is an outward sign of an inward work
4. Water-baptism portrays the union we have with Christ
5. Water-baptism is best fully immersed in the name of the Father, the Son, and the Holy Spirit
6. Water-baptism is a watery grave where we leave our sins and begin a new level of sanctification

If you are saved but have never been water-baptized, I am encouraging you to be water-baptized in 2022.

GET BAPTIZED IN 2022

Revelation 22

Revelation 22 is the final and last chapter of the Bible. What is pretty cool is that the Bible ends the way it begins. The Word of God comes full circle. The Bible begins with the beauty of the garden of Eden and ends talking about the beauty of the New Jerusalem. John gives us a detailed description of what we can look for during Jesus' millennial reign.

Description of New Jerusalem

1. A river of life that is crystal clear, v. 1
2. The tree of life, v. 2a
3. Twelve different fruits, v. 2b
   It is like we have a subscription to the fruit of the month club, as the tree of life will bear a different fruit each month.
4. Leaves that bring healing, v. 2c
5. No curses allowed, v. 3a
6. The throne of God, v. 3b
7. The Lamb of God, v. 3c
8. The righteous will be God's servants, v. 3d
9. No lamps and no sun will be needed because Jesus will be all the light we need, v. 5

Wow!!!! What a beautiful place to spend eternity. John goes on to give a few last instructions for us to grab ahold of before the end.

"And he said unto me, These sayings are faithful and true: and the Lord God of

the holy prophets sent his angel to shew
unto his servants the things which must
shortly be done." Revelation 22:6

God's Final Instructions

1. Prepare for the soon coming of Jesus,
   v. 7,12,20
   Three times in the last ten verses we are told
   to open our eyes and look because Jesus is
   coming soon.

2. Worship God, v. 8-9

3. There is a reward for the faithful based on
   our works on earth, v. 12

4. We are reminded Jesus is the Alpha and
   Omega, v. 13
   Jesus always was, always is, and always will
   be.

5. Righteousness is required to stay in the inner
   circle of God, v. 14-15

6. Jesus is the Root, the Offspring of David,
   and the Bright Morning Star, v. 16

7. When you are thirsty, come drink freely of the Water of Life, v. 17

8. Never add or subtract from God's Word, v. 18-19

9. The favor of the Lord is upon God's people, v. 21

What a wonderful way to end the best book ever written. Basically, what is happening is that the righteous have won!!! A result of us enduring and winning is that we are rewarded with eternal life.

"For the wages of sin is death; but the gift of God is eternal life through Jesus Christ our Lord." Romans 6:23

SERVING JESUS MAKES US WINNERS IN 2022

Chapter 22's Summary

Genesis 22   = Testing our Faith

Exodus 22   = Fulfill Your Social Responsibility

Leviticus 22   = Follow Priestly Guidelines

Numbers 22   = Be Smarter than a Donkey

Deuteronomy 22   = Honor Your Marriage

Joshua 22   = Seek Peaceful Resolutions

1 Samuel 22   = Have the Heart of God

2 Samuel 22   = Write Your Song

1 Kings 22   = Speak the Truth

2 Kings 22   = Train the Children

1 Chronicles 22   = Be A Watchman

2 Chronicles 22   = Listen Only to Godly Advice

Job 22   = Reject Stubbornness

Psalm 22   = Carry Your Cross

Proverbs 22   = Commit to Better Yourself

Isaiah 22   = Trust God, Not Man

Jeremiah 22   = Still Time to Change

Ezekiel 22   = Stand Up and Speak out for God

Matthew 22   = An Open Invitation to Come to Jesus

Luke 22   = Guard Against Betrayal

Acts 22   = Get Baptized

Revelation 22   = Serving Jesus Makes Us Winners

CHAPTER 6
Spiritual Forecast

Every year God gives me a prophetic Word for our nation. This Word is a spiritual forecast for what lies ahead for the United States of America. When God gave me the word for America for this year it was at one o'clock in the morning, as I was suffering with a kidney stone. In other words, this word was birthed in great pain. This is not going to be an easy year, and this is a sobering word to read. Just know that God will never leave us and never forsake. It may be a difficult word to swallow so keep chewing until you can break it down and have it go down smoother.

Prophetic Word for 2022

You have eyes to see, yet you are blind. You have ears to hear, but you do not listen. You have a mouth to speak; however, you are silent. You have a mind to think, but you have shut out common sense from the scriptures. You have ignored My pleas and chosen to follow others down a path of destruction because of peer pressure in society. You are not discerning the signs of the times, and you are forgetting the spiritual lessons you have been taught. The elect are being deceived and are falling into an inescapable trap. You have allowed the media around you and the fear within you to desensitize your own spirit to the point where you excuse away your own disobedience to the written Word. What used to bother you in the past no longer affects you in the present. You are motivated by your own personal agendas and have become people that fit in with the crowd instead of standing out among the crowd. You have compromised and lowered the standard of righteousness. You have wandered far from your First Love. You have developed your own set of rules based upon feeling, not truth. You have trusted science and technology more than you have had faith in God. You have listened to ungodly people more than you have listened to God. You have fallen asleep while you were supposed to be on active duty. You are spiritual MIA's. You are missing in action in the army of God. Even as you read this prophetic Word, you will judge it as if it were from man and not from God. You will read into the prophetic Word based on your own human intellect and make excuses as to why it is not for you. STOP IT!!!! Stop running away from the truth and accept this Word as the Word for the hour. As I the Lord called out and asked in the garden, "Adam, where are you?," I'm calling out to My people in 2022 and asking, "Where are you?" Where are you when you are needed the most? My coming is soon ... WAKE UP!!!

These are the 22 Signs of My Soon Coming

1. Increase in wars and rumors of wars, Matthew 24:6-7a
2. Famines, Matthew 24:7b
3. Pandemics, Matthew 24:7b
4. Earthquakes, Matthew 24:7b
5. Extreme materialism, 2 Timothy 3:1-2
6. Disobedient children, 2 Timothy 3:2
7. Departure from faith/false teachers, 1 Timothy 4:1
8. Unification of the world's religious, political, and economical systems, Revelation 13:4-8
9. Universal drug usage, Revelation 9:21
10. Abnormal sexual activity, Romans 1:17-32
11. Unnatural affections, 2 Timothy 3:3
12. Widespread violence, Revelation 9:21
13. People without a conscience, 1 Timothy 4:2
14. Rejection of God's Word, 2 Timothy 4:3-4
15. False claims of peace, 1 Thess. 5:1-3
16. Rise of false prophets, Matthew 24:5,11
17. Deception, Mark 13:5-6
18. Global warming, Revelation 16:8-9
19. Jews returning to homeland, Isaiah 43:5-6
20. Increase of anti-Semitism, Zechariah 14:2
21. Chaotic weather patterns, Luke 21:25
22. Gospel preached around the world, Matthew 24:14

This is not the first time you have heard these truths. Despite your disobedience and My frustration with you, there is still time, but time is running out. My patience is wearing thin. There are four things that must be done immediately:

1. Repent of your sins
2. Return to your First Love
3. Repeat your initial obedience
4. Report for active service

This year of 2022 will bring unprecedented evil and unapparelled deception. The devil is always subtle, and sin always evolves slowly. You must be wise as serpents and allow the Holy Spirit to guide your every step. The enemy will continue to lie to you about how life should be fair, and he will tempt you to entertain things that will only lead to destruction. The devil wants you to make decisions that will isolate you as you partake in the stinking-thinking mentality of "if it feels good, then just do it." The devil wants you to blame God when things go wrong, and question whether or not God truly loves you. The enemy does not want you to connect with the Lord and have a relationship with God. The devil's goal is to separate, isolate, and annihilate. Instead, stay connected to the Lord and to your God-sends. Grab ahold and do not let go of what God has established in your life. Do not allow a doubling of the delusion that is coming this year to derail you off your God-inspired course. Stay true to the Word of God and let the Holy Spirit guide you into all truth. This year will not be easy, and in many ways, it will not be fair, but with God on your side, you will make it through. Stop being a people-pleaser and start being a God-pleaser. You cannot have one foot in the world and one foot in the Lord in 2022 because it will not be tolerated by either side. Make up your mind and run straight ahead to victory toward the finish line in 2022!

In the next few pages, I break down the United States into five regions. Each region has a specific landmark, state, and large city to watch. It will give you a book of the Bible to read from, a prayer to pray, and months to watch closely to see what God is doing. Find where your state is and read the specifics. Keep these in mind as you continue to pray for those things in your region. Journal in the section I provided of anything the Lord shows you corelating with these things or times.

The Five Regions of the United States

West	Southwest	Midwest	Southeast	Northeast
Alaska	Arizona	Illinois	Alabama	Connecticut
California	Arkansas	Indiana	Florida	Delaware
Hawaii	Colorado	Iowa	Georgia	Maine
Idaho	Louisiana	Kansas	Kentucky	Maryland
Montana	New Mexico	Michigan	Mississippi	Massachusettes
Nevada	Oklahoma	Minnesota	North Carolina	New Hampshire
Oregon	Texas	Missouri	South Carolina	New Jersey
Utah		Nebraska	Tennessee	New York
Washington		North Dakota	Virginia	Pennsylvania
Wyoming		Ohio	West Virginia	Rhode Island
		South Dakota		Vermont
		Wisconsin		

West Region

States in the West Region and Their Specific "Word" for 2022:

Alaska – Desire

California – Master

Hawaii – Protection

Idaho – Openness

Montana – Update

Nevada – Activate

Oregon – Peace

Utah – Support

Washington – Vision

Wyoming – Generosity

Prayer for the West Region:

Strengthen what is weak, mend what is broken, bind what is bruised, heal what is sick, and resurrect what is dead. Give me life to live!!

Book of the Bible for the West Region:

Proverbs

Scripture for the West Region:

"It is of the Lord's mercies that we are not consumed, because his compassions fail not. They are new every morning:

great is thy faithfulness." Lamentations 3:22-23

West Region Landmark to Watch:
Golden Gate Bridge

State in the West Region to Watch:
Hawaii

Major City in the West Region to Watch:
Los Angeles, California

Key Months for the West Region:
March, May, August, and October

Southwest Region

States in the Southwest Region and Their Specific "Word" for 2022:
Arizona – Plant
Arkansas – Healing
Colorado – Explore
Louisiana – Unify
New Mexico – Reconciliation
Oklahoma – Love
Texas – Boldness

Prayer for the Southwest Region:
May the will of God guide me. May the light of God shine through me. May the power of God protect me. May the strength of God uphold me. May the mind of God rule me. May the love of God encourage me. May the joy of God uplift me.

Book of the Bible for the Southwest Region:
Acts

Scripture for the Southwest Region:

> *"The Lord is good, a strong hold in the day of trouble; and he knoweth them that trust in him." Nahum 1:7*

Southwest Region Landmark to Watch:
Hot Springs National Park

State in the Southwest Region to Watch:
Arizona

Major City in the Southwest Region to Watch:
Denver, Colorado

Key Months for the Southwest Region:
January, June, and September

Midwest Region

States in the Midwest Region and Their Specific "Word" for 2022:

Illinois – Capitalize

Indiana – Yield

Iowa – Transformation

Kansas – Training

Michigan – Hope

Minnesota – Test

Missouri – Simplify

Nebraska – Promotion

North Dakota – Wisdom

Ohio – Investigate

South Dakota – Meditate

Wisconsin – Passion

Prayer for the Midwest Region:

I pray against the thoughts that haunt me, the fears that control me, the lies that deceive me, and the sadness that depresses me. I plead the blood of Jesus over my life.

Book of the Bible for the Midwest Region:

1 Kings

Scripture for the Midwest Region:

> *"Come unto me, all ye that labour and are heavy laden, and I will give you rest." Matthew 11:28*

Midwest Region Landmark to Watch:
Navy Pier

State in the Midwest Region to Watch:
Iowa

Major City in the Midwest Region to Watch:
St. Paul, Minnesota

Key Months for the Midwest Region:
February, May, August, and December

Southeast Region

States in the Southeast Region and Their Specific "Word" for 2022:
Alabama – Gentleness
Florida – Encouragement
Georgia – Victory
Kentucky – Discipline
Mississippi – Empathy

North Carolina – Revival
South Carolina – Contentment
Tennessee – Praise
Virginia – Joy
West Virginia – Opportunity

Prayer for the Southeast Region:
Cancel and destroy every weapon formed against me in the name of Jesus, and I declare the enemy cannot curse what God has already blessed.

Book of the Bible for the Southeast Region:
Ecclesiastes

Scripture for the Southeast Region:

> *"Thou wilt keep him in perfect peace, whose mind is stayed on thee: because he trusteth in thee."* Isaiah 26:3

Southeast Region Landmark to Watch:
Blue Ridge Parkway

State in the Southeast Region to Watch:
North Carolina

Major City in the Southeast Region to Watch:
Atlanta, Georgia

Key Months for the Southeast Region:
April, July, and November

Northeast Region

States in the Northeast Region and Their Specific "Word" for 2022:
Connecticut – Faith
Delaware – Discernment
Maine – Openness
Maryland – Strength
Massachusetts – Prosperity
New Hampshire – Courage
New Jersey – Fervent
New York – Trust
Pennsylvania – Grace
Rhode Island – Balance
Vermont – Dependable

Prayer for the Northeast Region:
I am the head and not the tail, the blessed and not the cursed, the chosen not the rejected, the free and not the bound, the rich and not the poor, and the victor, not the victim.

Book of the Bible for the Northeast Region:
Genesis

Scripture for the Northeast Region:

> *"He only is my rock and my salvation:*
> *he is my defence; I shall not be moved."*
> *Psalm 62:6*

Northeast Region Landmark to Watch:
Lincoln Memorial

State in the Northeast Region to Watch:
Maryland

Major City in the Northeast Region to Watch:
Camden, New Jersey

Key Months for the Northeast Region:
January, March, June, and October

It is incumbent upon the Church to pray for our Nation. America needs prayer. Our country will face great challenges in 2022 and the best way for us to win the battle is on our knees in prayer.

Let's Intercede for our Nation!

CHAPTER 7
Characteristics of 22nd Day People

This year will be a time when your inner inspiration and outward motivation will be at an all-time high. Your inspiration and motivation will lead to realization in 2022. Use your intellect and instincts in reaching your goals and fulfilling your dreams. You must combine patience and persistent for success to be manifested. Listen to those who push you and even provoke you to be more than you think is possible.

You have always been a unique and original individual. You have handled situations with poise and grace. You have approached problems systematically and have had high ambitions. You are orderly and perceptive. There are a lot of great qualities that abound in your life. However, there are some areas that need to be improved in order for you to go to the next level. You cannot take everything so personal and must stop letting your intellect get in the way of your faith in God. You are smart, but not smarter than God. You can be stubborn when you get an idea in your head. So, it is important that you follow the Holy Spirit to soften your heart to become more pliable. Beware of people who are bad influences and who try to take advantage of your kindness. Do not let anyone or anything get in your way.

Five Keys to Success in 2022

1. Set goals that are reasonable and reachable
2. Do not rush to judgement
3. Always put family first
4. Be more flexible
5. Trust the Lord more than yourself

Character Traits of 22nd Day People

Positive	Negative
- Respectful	- Emotional
- Instinctive	- Spontaneous
- Hard workers	- Hard on yourself
- Organized	- Big talker
- Overachievers	- Suspicious
- Self-motivated	- Frustrated easily
- Multi-faceted	- Angry
- Visionaries	- Fanatical
- Motivates others	- Pessimistic
- Good discernment	- Great internal pressure to succeed
- Charismatic	- Not the best at handling disappointment

Favorite Color: Red

Best Day: Sundays

Best Month: April

Scripture: Proverbs 3:5-6

I have created a list of just some of the famous celebrities who were born on the 22nd day of each month.

JANUARY 22nd

Charles White, Football Hall of Famer
Guy Fieri, Chef
Steve Perry, Rock Singer
DJ Jazzy Jeff, DJ
Linda Blair, Actress
Ray Rice, NFL Player

FEBRUARY 22nd

George Washington, 1st President of the USA
Steve Irwin, Reality Star
Drew Barrymore, Actress
Julius Erving, Basketball
Ted Kennedy, Politician
Sparky Anderson, MLB Manager

MARCH 22nd

Reese Witherspoon, Actress
JJ Watt, NFL Player
William Shatner, Actor
Rick Harrison, Reality Star
Andrew Lloyd Webber, Composer

APRIL 22nd

Machine Gun Kelly, Rapper
Marshawn Lynch, NFL Player
Jack Nicholson, Actor
Willie Robertson, Reality Star
Glen Campbell, Country Singer

MAY 22nd

Naomi Campbell, Model
Daniel Bryan, Wrestler
Julian Edelman, NFL Player
Maggie Q, Actress
Sean Gunn, Actor
Arthur Conan Doyle, Author of Sherlock Holmes

JUNE 22nd

Meryl Streep, Actress
Cyndi Lauper, Pop Singer
Elizabeth Warren, Politician
Carson Daly, TV Show Host
Pete Maravich, NBA Player
Clyde Drexler, NBA Player
Kurt Warner, NFL Hall of Famer

JULY 22nd

Selena Gomez, Singer/Actress
Prince George, British Royalty
Alex Trebek, Game Show Host
Shawn Michaels, Wrestler
David Spade, Actor
Ezekiel Elliott, NFL Player
Willem Dafoe, Actor
Danny Glover, Actor
John Leguizamo, Actor

AUGUST 22nd

James Corden, Comedian
Jimmy Uso, Wrestler
Jey Uso, Wrestler
Kristen Wiig, Actress
Bill Parcells, NFL Coach

SEPTEMBER 22nd

Joan Jett, Singer
Scott Baio, Actor
Andrea Bocelli, Opera Singer
Tommy Lasorda, Baseball Manager
Bonnie Hunt, Actress
Billie Piper, Singer

OCTOBER 22nd

TobyMac, Christian Rapper
Jeff Goldblum, Actor
Shaggy, Singer
Christopher Lloyd, Actor
Annette Funicello, Actress

NOVEMBER 22nd

Scarlett Johanson, Actress
Hailey (Baldwin) Bieber, Model
Mark Ruffalo, Actor
JuJu Smith-Schuster, NFL Player
Jamie Lee Curtis, Actress
Billie Jean King, Tennis Player
Michael D. Cohen, Actor

DECEMBER 22nd

Meghan Trainor, Pop Singer
DaBaby, Rapper
Ted Cruz, Politician
Maurice Gibb, Singer
Robin Gibb, Singer

Prophetic Word for People born on the 22nd Day of the Month

This will be an incredible year for expansion and increase in your life. Make sure you stay out of the bushes and walk in integrity. There will be a lot of chaos around you, but steer clear of all disorder. Allow God to bring you closer to people who are your God-sends and separate you from people who are the thorns in your flesh. Make sure your steps are ordered of the Lord as the Holy Spirit directs and guides you. These are your marching orders so, step into your destiny and enjoy success in 2022.

CHAPTER 8
Scriptural References

The Top 20:22 Scriptures for 2022

"And the LORD said unto Moses, Thus thou shalt say unto the children of Israel, Ye have seen that I have talked with you from heaven." Exodus 20:22

"Ye shall therefore keep all my statutes, and all my judgments, and do them: that the land, whither I bring you to dwell therein, spue you not out." Leviticus 20:22

"And the people the men of Israel encouraged themselves, and set their battle again in array in the place where they put themselves in array the first day." Judges 20:22

"And when they began to sing and to praise, the Lord set ambushments against the children of Ammon, Moab,

and mount Seir, which were come against Judah; and they were smitten." 2 Chronicles 20:22

"Say not thou, I will recompense evil; but wait on the Lord, and he shall save thee." Proverbs 20:22

"Is it lawful for us to give tribute unto Caesar, or no?" Luke 20:22

"And when he had said this, he breathed on them, and saith unto them, Receive ye the Holy Ghost:" John 20:22

The Top 22:22 Scriptures for 2022

"Ye shall not afflict any widow, or fatherless child." Exodus 22:22

"Blind, or broken, or maimed, or having a wen, or scurvy, or scabbed, ye shall not offer these unto the Lord, nor make

an offering by fire of them upon the altar unto the Lord." Leviticus 22:22

"For I have kept the ways of the Lord, and have not wickedly departed from my God." 2 Samuel 22:22

"Receive, I pray thee, the law from his mouth, and lay up his words in thine heart." Job 22:22

"I will declare thy name unto my brethren: in the midst of the congregation will I praise thee." Psalm 22:22

"Rob not the poor, because he is poor: neither oppress the afflicted in the gate:" Proverbs 22:22

"And the key of the house of David will I lay upon his shoulder; so he shall open, and none shall shut; and he shall shut, and none shall open." Isaiah 22:22

"And truly the Son of man goeth, as it was determined: but woe unto that man by whom he is betrayed!" Luke 22:22

"And they gave him audience unto this word, and then lifted up their voices, and said, Away with such a fellow from the earth: for it is not fit that he should live." Acts 22:22

Nine Scripture References with the Number 22

"Ummah also, and Aphek, and Rehob: twenty and two cities with their villages." Joshua 19:30

"And after him arose Jair, a Gileadite, and judged Israel twenty and two years." Judges 10:3

"And the days which Jeroboam reigned were two and twenty years: and he slept with his fathers, and Nadab his son reigned in his stead." 1 Kings 14:20

"And in the thirty and eighth year of Asa king of Judah began Ahab the son of Omri to reign over Israel: and Ahab the son of Omri reigned over Israel in Samaria twenty and two years." 1 Kings 16:29

"Two and twenty years old was Ahaziah when he began to reign; and he reigned one year in Jerusalem. And his mother's name was Athaliah, the daughter of Omri king of Israel." 2 Kings 8:26

"Amon was twenty and two years old when he began to reign, and he reigned two years in Jerusalem. And his mother's name was Meshullemeth, the daughter of Haruz of Jotbah." 2 Kings 21:19

"And Zadok, a young man mighty of valour, and of his father's house twenty and two captains."1 Chronicles 12:28

"But Abijah waxed mighty, and married fourteen wives, and begat twenty and

90

two sons, and sixteen daughters."
2 Chronicles 13:21

"Amon was two and twenty years old when he began to reign, and reigned two years in Jerusalem." 2 Chronicles 33:21

22 Scriptures for 2022

"For by him were all things created, that are in heaven, and that are in earth, visible and invisible, whether they be thrones, or dominions, or principalities, or powers: all things were created by him, and for him:" Colossians 1:16

"And the Spirit and the bride say, Come. And let him that heareth say, Come. And let him that is athirst come. And whosoever will, let him take the water of life freely." Revelation 22:17

"The fear of the Lord tendeth to life: and he that hath it shall abide satisfied; he

shall not be visited with evil." Proverbs 19:23

"Love not the world, neither the things that are in the world. If any man love the world, the love of the Father is not in him." 1 John 2:15

"Nevertheless let every one of you in particular so love his wife even as himself; and the wife see that she reverence her husband." Ephesians 5:33

"She openeth her mouth with wisdom; and in her tongue is the law of kindness." Proverbs 31:26

"He that believeth on me, as the scripture hath said, out of his belly shall flow rivers of living water." John 7:38

"But the fruit of the Spirit is love, joy, peace, longsuffering, gentleness, goodness, faith, Meekness, temperance:

92

against such there is no law." Galatians 5:22-23

"For to one is given by the Spirit the word of wisdom; to another the word of knowledge by the same Spirit; To another faith by the same Spirit; to another the gifts of healing by the same Spirit; To another the working of miracles; to another prophecy; to another discerning of spirits; to another divers kinds of tongues; to another the interpretation of tongues:" 1 Corinthians 12:8-10

"Therefore they that were scattered abroad went every where preaching the word. Then Philip went down to the city of Samaria, and preached Christ unto them. And the people with one accord gave heed unto those things which Philip spake, hearing and seeing the miracles which he did." Acts 8:4-6

"And whosoever of you will be the chiefest, shall be servant of all." Mark 10:44

"But ye are a chosen generation, a royal priesthood, an holy nation, a peculiar people; that ye should shew forth the praises of him who hath called you out of darkness into his marvellous light;"1 Peter 2:9

"Let all things be done decently and in order." 1 Corinthians 14:40

And Ruth said, Intreat me not to leave thee, or to return from following after thee: for whither thou goest, I will go; and where thou lodgest, I will lodge: thy people shall be my people, and thy God my God: Where thou diest, will I die, and there will I be buried: the Lord do so to me, and more also, if ought but death part thee and me." Ruth 1:16-17

"I was glad when they said unto me, Let us go into the house of the Lord." Psalm 122:1

"My brethren, count it all joy when ye fall into divers temptations;" James 1:2

"These things I have spoken unto you, that in me ye might have peace. In the world ye shall have tribulation: but be of good cheer; I have overcome the world." John 16:33

"Let all your things be done with charity." 1 Corinthians 16:14

"For where envying and strife is, there is confusion and every evil work." James 3:16

"What therefore God hath joined together, let not man put asunder." Mark 10:9

"Nevertheless I have somewhat against thee, because thou hast left thy first love." Revelation 2:4

"And as ye would that men should do to you, do ye also to them likewise." Luke 6:31

CHAPTER 9
2022 Calendar

JANUARY

- National Blood Donor Month
- National Hobby Month
- National Hot Tea Month
- National Slavery and Human Trafficking Prevention Month
- National Soup Month

Jan 1   - New Year's Day
Jan 6   - Epiphany
Jan 17 - Martin Luther King Jr. Day

FEBRUARY

- American Heart Month
- Black History Month
- National Bake for Family Fun Month
- National Hot Breakfast Month
- National Library Lover's Month
- National Snack Food Month

Feb 1 - Chinese New Year
Feb 1 - National Freedom Day

Feb 2   - Groundhog Day
Feb 4   - Rosa Parks Day
Feb 4   - National Wear Red Day
Feb 12 - President Lincoln's Birthday
Feb 13 - Super Bowl
Feb 14 - Valentine's Day
Feb 15 - Susan B. Anthony's Birthday
Feb 21 - Presidents' Day

MARCH

- Irish American Heritage Month
- Multiple Sclerosis Awareness Month
- National Caffeine Awareness Month
- National Brain Injury Awareness Month
- National Nutrition Month
- Women's Awareness Month

Mar 1   - Fat Tuesday/Mardi Gras
Mar 2   - Ash Wednesday
Mar 2   - Read Across America Day
Mar 4   - Employee Appreciation Day
Mar 13 - Daylight Saving Time starts
Mar 16 - Purim begins
Mar 17 - St. Patrick's Day
Mar 20 - Spring Begins
Mar 29 - Vietnam War Veterans Day

APRIL

- National Month of Hope
- Distracted Driving Awareness Month
- National Child Abuse Awareness Month
- Keep America Beautiful Month
- National Autism Awareness Month
- National Parkinson's Awareness Month
- National Pecan Month
- National Volunteer Month

Apr 10 - Palm Sunday
Apr 12 - Library Workers' Day
Apr 13 - Thomas Jefferson's Birthday
Apr 14 - Maundy Thursday
Apr 15 - Good Friday
Apr 15 - Passover (first day)
Apr 16 - Holy Saturday
Apr 17 - Easter Sunday
Apr 18 - Tax Deadline
Apr 18 - Boston Marathon
Apr 23 - Passover (last day)
Apr 27 - Administrative Professionals Day
Apr 28 - Take your Child to Work Day
Apr 29 - Arbor Day

MAY

- National Dental Care Month
- National Military Appreciation Month
- National Motorcycle Awareness Month
- Date Your Mate Month
- National Barbecue Month
- National Blood Pressure Month
- National Hamburger Month

May 4 - Kent State Shootings Remembrance
May 5 - Cinco de Mayo
May 5 - National Day of Prayer
May 6 - Kentucky Oaks
May 6 - National Nurses Day
May 6 - Military Spouse Appreciation Day
May 7 - Kentucky Derby
May 8 - Mother's Day
May 15 - Peace Officers Memorial Day
May 21 - Armed Forces Day
May 25 - Emergency Medical Services for
          Children Day
May 25 - National Missing Children's Day
May 26 - Ascension Day
May 30 - Memorial Day

JUNE

- Aquarium Month
- Men's Health Month
- National Fresh Fruit and Vegetables Month
- National Candy Month
- National Great Outdoors Month

Jun 4 - Shavuot
Jun 5 - Pentecost
Jun 6 - D-Day
Jun 11 - Belmont Stakes
Jun 12 - Trinity Sunday
Jun 12 - Bunker Hill Day
Jun 14 - Army Birthday
Jun 14 - Flag Day
Jun 19 - Juneteenth
Jun 19 - Father's Day
Jun 20 - American Eagle Day
Jun 21 - Summer Begins

JULY

- National Baked Bean Month
- National Cell Phone Courtesy Month
- National Hot Dog Month
- National Ice Cream Month
- National Picnic Month

Jul 4 - Independence Day

Jul 24 - Parents' Day

Jul 27 - Korean War Veterans Armistice Day

AUGUST

- National Wellness Month
- Family Fun Month
- National Eye Exam Month
- National Golf Month
- National Sandwich Month

Aug 4 - Coast Guard Birthday

Aug 7 - Purple Heart Day

Aug 19 - National Aviation Day

Aug 21 - Senior Citizens Day

Aug 26 - Women's Equality Day

SEPTEMBER

- Baby Safety Month
- Classical Music Month
- National Potato Month
- National Preparedness Month
- National Suicide Prevention Month

Sep 5 - Labor Day

Sep 11 - Patriot Day

Sep 11 - National Grandparents Day

Sep 16 - POW/MIA Recognition Day

Sep 17 - Constitution Day & Citizenship Day

Sep 17 - National Clean Up Day

Sep 18 - Air Force Birthday

Sep 22 - Fall Begins

Sep 23 - Native Americans' Day

Sep 25 - Rosh Hashana

OCTOBER

- American Cheese Month
- Breast Cancer Awareness Month
- Church Safety and Security Month
- Financial Planning Month
- National Book Month
- National Dessert Month

Oct 3 - Child Health Day

Oct 4 - Yom Kippur

Oct 9 - First Day of Sukkot

Oct 10 - Columbus Day

Oct 13 - Navy Birthday

Oct 15 - Sweetest Day

Oct 16 - Last Day of Sukkot

Oct 17 - Boss' Day observed
Oct 18 - Simchat Torah
Oct 31 - Halloween

NOVEMBER
- National Adoption Month
- National Diabetes Month
- National Peanut Butter Lovers Month
- NoSHAVEmber (US – Beard Month)

Nov 1 - All Saints' Day
Nov 2 - All Souls' Day
Nov 6 - Daylight Saving Time Ends
Nov 6 - New York City Marathon
Nov 10 - Marine Corps Birthday
Nov 11 - Veterans Day
Nov 24 - Thanksgiving Day
Nov 25 - Black Friday
Nov 27 - First Sunday of Advent
Nov 28 - Cyber Monday

DECEMBER
- AIDS Awareness Month
- National Human Rights Month
- Spiritual Literacy Month

Dec 1 - Rosa Parks Day

Dec 7 - Pearl Harbor Remembrance Day

Dec 13 - National Guard Birthday

Dec 18 - First Day of Chanukah/Hanukkah

Dec 21 - Winter Begins

Dec 24 - Christmas Eve

Dec 25 - Christmas Day

Dec 26 - Last Day of Chanukah/Hanukkah

Dec 31 - New Year's Eve

CHAPTER 10
Journal

Journaling is one way to look back on, and remind us of, the miracle working power of God in our lives. In Matthew 16, Jesus encouraged His disciples to journal and document the miracles they saw in order to remain strong and not lose faith. It is important that we write blessings down, and document important dates and events to encourage ourselves when the enemy wants us to forget the greatness of God. This chapter is to log such events. When you hear the number 22 mentioned, document where, when, and why it was mentioned. See if it has any significance to the vision cast out for 2022. You will be surprised by how many times this number is going to pop up when you are paying attention and sensitive to hearing it on TV, radio, newspaper articles, etc. At the end of the year, you will hopefully have a couple sheets of paper to help you judge whether the prophetic message of this book has been relevant in your life and in the world.

Here are the 22 dates the Lord spoke to me to be on the lookout for something:

1. Sunday, January 2, 2022

_____

_____

_____

2. Monday, January 17, 2022

_____

_____

_____

3. Wednesday, February 2, 2022

_____

_____

_____

4. Thursday, February 24, 2022

_____

_____

_____

5. Tuesday, March 8, 2022

_____

_____

_____

6. Wednesday, March 30, 2022

_____

_____

_____

7. Saturday, April 9, 2022

_____

_____

_____

8. Friday, April 29, 2022

_____

_____

_____

9. Sunday, May 8, 2022

_____

_____

_____

10.Saturday, May 28, 2022

_____

_____

_____

11.Wednesday, June 15, 2022

_____

_____

_____

12. Thursday, June 30, 2022

_____

_____

_____

13. Monday, July 4, 2022

_____

_____

_____

14. Saturday, July 30, 2022

_____

_____

_____

15. Tuesday, August 9, 2022

_____

_____

_____

16. Saturday, August 20, 2022

_____

_____

_____

17. Sunday, September 11, 2022

_____

_____

_____

18. Saturday, October 8, 2022

_____

_____

_____

19. Monday, October 31, 2022

_____

_____

_____

20. Friday, November 11, 2022

_____

_____

_____

21. Friday, November 25, 2022

_____

_____

_____

22. Wednesday, December 21, 2022

_____

_____

_____

Write out any other dates that may mean something to you:

Date   Notes

_____

_____

_____

_____

_____

_____

_____

_____

_____

_____

_____

_____

_____

_____

_____

_____

_____

_____

_____

_____

_____

_____

_____

_____

Date   Notes

Date   Notes

Date   Notes

CONCLUSION

It is the end of the book but the beginning of the personal application process. Wisdom is what we need in 2022, and wisdom means that you are applying the learned knowledge to your everyday life. This is not going to be an easy year, but we have a promise from God in scripture that we must hold onto throughout this year.

> *"These things I have spoken unto you, that in me ye might have peace. In the world ye shall have tribulation: but be of good cheer; I have overcome the world." John 16:33*

The vision has been written and released, so run with what you have. You may wish you would have been dealt another hand of cards, but you have to work with what you got. There is a lot to digest but take the time to swallow the truth. The knowledge of the truth is what is going to set you free and help you keep your faith.

If you are married, seek to improve your marriage. If you are single, do not get married until you are equally yoked with your God-send. Improve yourself by connecting with God first; then you will be ready to connect with someone else. Keep your head up because everything that can be shaken will be shaken in 2022. You were born to win, so keep your eyes on God to stay a winner. The deception, delusion, and darkness of the enemy may double, but the attack of the devil always attracts the anointing of the Holy Spirit. God will guide you and direct you in 2022.

22 Guidelines for Success in 2022

1. Never doubt God
2. Keep your head up
3. Smile
4. Make good friends
5. Pray through
6. Excel in excellence
7. Love life
8. Give more hugs
9. Meditate on the Word
10. Do not be rude
11. Exercise more
12. Love everybody
13. Study the Word
14. Go to the church more
15. Appreciate the little things
16. Think positive
17. Eat better
18. Be nicer

19. Witness more
20. Reject racism
21. Forgive others
22. Be patient

"Nay, in all these things we are more than conquerors through him that loved us." Romans 8:37

YOU WILL WIN IN 2022!!

To get daily wisdom nuggets, check out Pastor Bill on social media for the most important minute of your day!

The Minute That Matters

Tik Tok

@pbilljenkins   @pastorbillj   Pastor Bill Jenkins

Pastor Bill Jenkins   Pastor Bill Jenkins

Scan the QR code with your phone and you will be automatically connected to your choice of social media.

CPSIA information can be obtained
at www.ICGtesting.com
Printed in the USA
BVHW040908091221
623624BV00012B/252

9 780578 327365